Materials

The following materials are recommended for preparing your fleece fabric strips and crocheting them:

- Cutting mat
- Rotary cutter
- Size 13 tapestry needle (with large eye)
- Fabric glue, such as Beacon FabriTac
- Scissors
- Fleece fabric yardage*
- Acrylic ruler
- Plastic crochet hook, such as Susan Bates Crystalites®

*Precut fabric, such as those from Cranston Fabri/Knit, can be used instead of cutting your own strips. It is available with fourteen 5-yard ¼-inch precut strips in each package.

Gauge

Gauge will vary depending on the thickness of the fabric strips, size of crochet hook and pattern stitch that is used. Be sure to use the hook size that gives you the gauge specified with your pattern.

Cutting Continuous Fabric Strips

Lay fabric flat on cutting mat, folded lengthwise, with selvages together and folded edge toward you. Using rotary cutter and acrylic ruler, cut from fold toward selvages, stopping at the desired strip width from selvages (Fig. A).

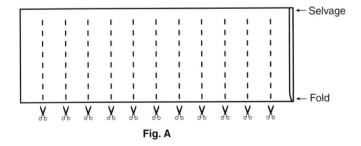

← Selvage

← Fold

Fig. A

Referring to Fig. B, unfold fabric and cut through selvage at every other cut on one side. On other side, cut through the selvage at alternate cuts from first side.

The thickness of the fleece will affect the weight of the finished yarn. Thinner fleece will approximate worsted weight yarn, while thick fleece will approximate bulky weight yarn. When cut into ½-inch or narrower strips the strip may roll in on itself while winding into a ball. Strips cut wider than ½ inch will remain flat.

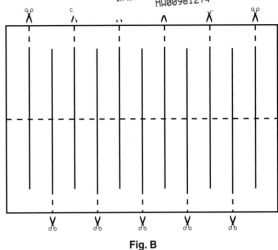

Fig. B

Hint

You may choose to cut the corners where the fabric "turns" so that they don't stick out of the finished project, Photo A.

Photo A

Using Precut Fabric Strips

When using precut 5-yard strips, it is not necessary to glue the ends together. You can tuck the ends into the already crocheted fabric after you are done. If you choose to glue the ends, use fabric glue sparingly.

Soft & Warm Slippers

EASY

Finished Sizes

Instructions given fit baby size; changes for child, small adult and medium adult sizes are in [ ].

Finished Measurements

Heel to toe: 4 [6, 8, 10] inches

Materials

For Baby Version
• Cranston Fabri/Knit precut fabric strips:
  32 yds mint
• Size L/11/8mm crochet hook or size needed to obtain gauge
• Tapestry needle
• Fabric glue

For Child Version
• Cranston Fabri/Knit precut fabric strips:
  35 yds each off-white and lavender
• Size L/11/8mm crochet hook or size needed to obtain gauge
• Tapestry needle
• Fabric glue

For Small Adult Version
• 27 x 60-inch piece of rainbow fleece
• Size L/11/8mm crochet hook or size needed to obtain gauge
• Tapestry needle
• Fabric glue

For Medium Adult Version
• Cranston Fabri/Knit precut fabric strips:
  85 yds light blue
• Size L/11/8mm crochet hook or size needed to obtain gauge
• Tapestry needle
• Fabric glue

Gauge

10 sc = 4 inches

Instructions

Slipper
Make 2.

Note: If using precut fleece strips, glue ends tog and roll in ball. If using rainbow fleece, cut a continuous strip ½-inch wide. For child version, alternate colors every 2 rows.

Row 1: Ch 13 [18, 23, 28]; sc in 2nd ch from hook and in each rem ch, turn. *(12 [17, 22, 27] sc)*

Row 2: Ch 1, sc in each sc, turn.

Rows 3–18 [20, 22, 24]: Rep row 2.

Row 19 [21, 23, 25]: Ch 1, working along next side in ends of rows, yo, draw up lp in each row, yo, draw through all lps on hook, turn.

Row 20 [22, 24, 26]: Working in unused lps of beg ch and through both lps of each st on last row at same time, sl st in first 6 [8, 10, 12] sts; sc in next 6 [9, 12, 15] sc in last row, sc in next 6 [9, 12, 15] unused lps of beg ch, turn. *(12 [18, 24, 30] sc)*

Row 21 [23, 25, 27]: Ch 1, sc in each sc.

Fasten off and weave in ends.

Assembly

Sew heel opening closed. With 10-inch strips of matching fleece, tie bow at center front of each Slipper.

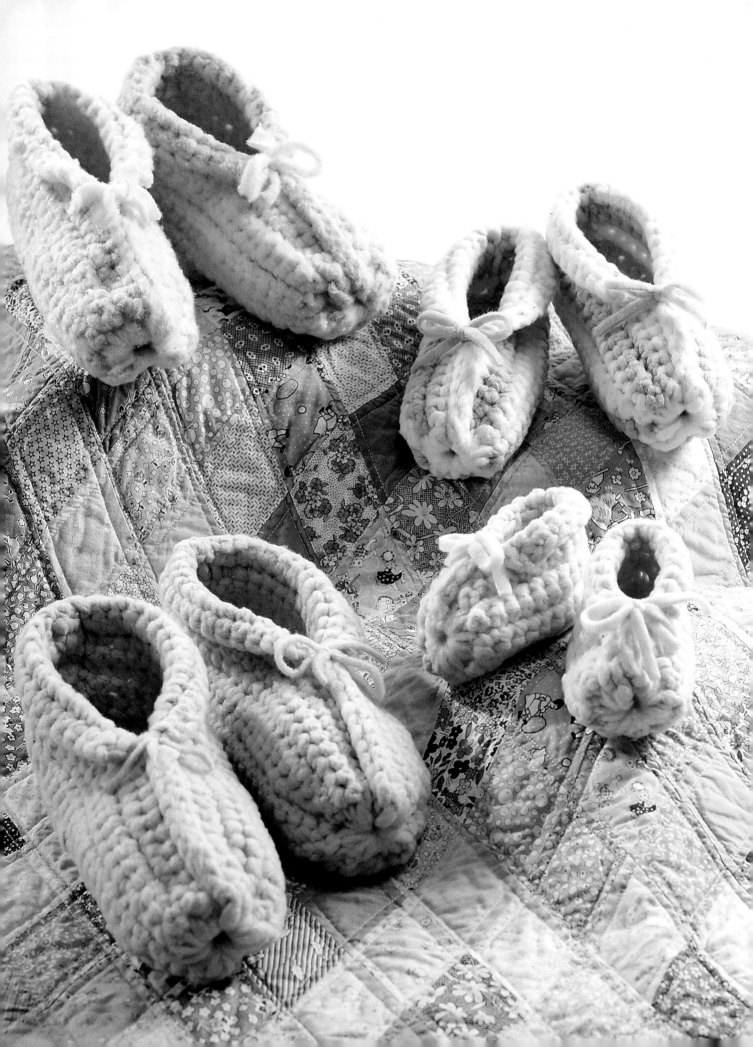

Comfy Dog Bed

EASY

Finished Size

18 x 28 inches

Materials

- 4¾ yds variegated brown fleece fabric
- Size L/11/8mm crochet hook or size needed to obtain gauge
- Tapestry needle
- 20 oz polyester fiberfill
- 1 standard-size pillow

Gauge

10 sts = 4 inches

Instructions

Top/Bottom

Make 2.

Rnd 1 (RS): Ch 31; sc in 2nd ch from hook and in each rem ch; working in unused lps on opposite side of beg ch, sc in next 29 lps. *(58 sc)*

Rnd 2: *2 sc in next sc; sc in next 2 sc, 2 sc in next sc; sc in next 10 sc, 2 sc in next sc; sc in next 10 sc, 2 sc in next sc; sc in next 2 sc, 2 sc in next sc; rep from * once more. *(68 sc)*

Rnd 3: *2 sc in next sc; sc in next 3 sc, 2 sc in next sc; sc in next 6 sc, 2 sc in next sc; sc in next 5 sc, 2 sc in next sc; sc in next 5 sc, 2 sc in next sc; sc in next 6 sc, 2 sc in next sc; sc in next 3 sc, 2 sc in next sc; rep from * once more. *(82 sc)*

Rnd 4: Sc in each sc.

Rnd 5: *2 sc in next sc; sc in next 4 sc, 2 sc in next sc; sc in next 6 sc, 2 sc in next sc; sc in next 7 sc, 2 sc in next sc; sc in next 7 sc, 2 sc in next sc; sc in next 6 sc, 2 sc in next sc; sc in next 4 sc, 2 sc in next sc; rep from * once more. *(96 sc)*

Rnd 6: *2 sc in next sc; sc in next 4 sc, 2 sc in next sc; sc in next 6 sc, 2 sc in next sc; sc in next 6 sc, 2 sc in next sc; sc in next 7 sc, 2 sc in next sc; sc in next 7 sc, 2 sc in next sc; sc in next 6 sc, 2 sc in next sc; sc in next 4 sc, 2 sc in next sc; rep from * once more. *(110 sc)*

Rnds 7 & 8: Rep rnd 4.

Rnd 9: *2 sc in next sc; sc in next 6 sc, 2 sc in next sc; sc in next 6 sc, 2 sc in next sc; sc in next 25 sc, 2 sc in next sc; sc in next 6 sc, 2 sc in next sc; sc in next 6 sc, 2 sc in next sc; rep from * once more. *(122 sc)*

Rnd 10: *2 sc in next sc; sc in next 7 sc, 2 sc in next sc; sc in next 7 sc, 2 sc in next sc; sc in next 26 sc, 2 sc in next sc; sc in next 7 sc, 2 sc in next sc; sc in next 7 sc, 2 sc in next sc; rep from * once more. *(134 sc)*

Rnds 11–13: Rep rnd 4.

Rnd 14: *2 sc in next sc; sc in next 8 sc, 2 sc in next sc; sc in next 9 sc, 2 sc in next sc; sc in next 27 sc, 2 sc in next sc; sc in next 9 sc, 2 sc in next sc; sc in next 8 sc, 2 sc in next sc; rep from * once more. *(146 sc)*

Rnd 15: *2 sc in next sc; sc in next 9 sc, 2 sc in next sc; sc in next 10 sc, 2 sc in next sc; sc in next 28 sc, 2 sc in next sc; sc in next 10 sc, 2 sc in next sc; sc in next 9 sc, 2 sc in next sc; rep from * once more. *(158 sc)*

Rnd 16: *[Sc in next 5 sc, 2 sc in next sc] 3 times; sc in next 40 sc, [sc in next 5 sc, 2 sc in next sc] 3 times; rep from * once more. *(170 sc)*

Rnd 17: Rep rnd 4.

Rnd 18: *[Sc in next 6 sc, 2 sc in next sc] 3 times; sc in next 42 sc, [sc in next 6 sc, 2 sc in next sc] 3 times; rep from * once more. *(182 sc)*

Rnd 19: *[Sc in next 7 sc, 2 sc in next sc] 3 times; sc in next 43 sc, [sc in next 7 sc, 2 sc in next sc] 3 times; rep from * once more. *(194 sc)*

Rnd 20: *[Sc in next 8 sc, 2 sc in next s] 3 times; sc in next 44 sc, [sc in next 8 sc, 2 sc in next sc] 3 times; rep from * once more. *(206 sc)*

Rnds 21 & 22: Rep rnd 4.

Fasten off and weave in ends.

Back Section

Row 1: Ch 31, sc in 2nd ch from hook and in each rem ch, turn. *(30 sc)*

Row 2: Ch 1, sc in each sc, turn.

Rows 3–118: Rep row 2.

Fasten off and weave in ends.

Finishing

Step 1: Sew long sides of Back Section tog; forming tube. Stuff with fiberfill, leaving ends slightly flatter, and sew each end closed.

Step 2: For bed, sew edges of Top and Bottom tog, inserting pillow before closing.

Step 3: Place center of Back Section at center of back of bed and sew seam side to bed, rounding corners and sewing ends of Back Section along sides of bed.

Cuddly Bear & Cub

EASY

Finished Sizes

Cub: 16 inches tall
Bear: 20 inches tall

Materials

For Cub

- Cranston Fabri/Knit precut fabric strips:
  3 packages #148 lavender
- Medium (worsted) weight yarn:
  small amount of black
- Size J/10/6mm crochet hook or size needed to
  obtain gauge
- Tapestry needle
- Polyester fiberfill

For Bear

- Heavyweight fleece fabric:
  ¼ yd each rainbow, green, yellow, lavender
- Size L/11/8mm crochet hook or size needed to
  obtain gauge
- Tapestry needle
- Polyester fiberfill

Gauge

Size J hook: 13 sc = 4 inches
Size L hook: 9 sc = 4 inches

Instructions

Note: *Pattern is written the same for both Cub and Bear. Hook size determines size of project. For Bear, change colors as desired.*

Head & Body

Note: *Head and Body are worked in continuous rnds. Do not join; mark beg of rnds.*

Rnd 1: With desired color, ch 4, join to form a ring; 8 sc in ring.

Rnd 2: 2 sc in each sc. *(16 sc)*

Rnd 3: Rep rnd 2. *(32 sc)*

Rnd 4: Sc in each sc.

Rnds 5–14: Rep rnd 4.

Rnd 15: [Sc in next 2 sc, sk next sc, sc in next sc] 8 times. *(24 sc)*

Rnd 16: [Sc in next sc, sk next sc, sc in next sc] 8 times. *(16 sc)*

Rnd 17: Rep rnd 4.

Rnd 18: 2 sc in each sc. *(32 sc)*

Rnds 19–28: Rep rnd 4.

Rnd 29: [Sc in next sc, 2 sc in next sc] 16 times. *(48 sc)*

Rnds 30–39: Rep rnd 4.

Stuff with fiberfill and shape.

Rnd 40: [Sc in next 2 sc, sk next sc, sc in next sc] 12 times. *(36 sc)*

Stuff with fiberfill.

Rnd 41: [Sc in next sc, sk next sc, sc in next sc] 12 times. *(24 sc)*

Rnd 42: [Sc in next sc, sk next sc, sc in next sc] 8 times. 24 sc. *(16 sc)*

Stuff with fiberfill and shape.

Rnd 43: [Sc in next sc, sk next sc] 8 times. *(8 sc)*

Rnd 44: [Sl st in next sc, sk next sc] 4 times. *(4 sl sts)*

Fasten off and weave in ends.

Front Leg
Make 2.

Note: Front Leg is worked in continuous rnds. Do not join; mark beg of rnds.

Rnd 1: Ch 4, join to form a ring; 2 sc in each ch. *(8 sc)*

Rnd 2: 2 sc in each sc. *(16 sc)*

Rnd 3: Sc in each sc.

Rnds 4–17: Rep rnd 3.

Stuff with fiberfill and shape.

Rnd 18: [Sc in next sc, sk next sc] 8 times. *(8 sc)*

Rnd 19: [Sl st in next sc, sk next sc] 4 times. *(4 sl sts)*

Fasten off and weave in ends.

Back Leg
Make 2.

Note: Back Leg is worked in continuous rnds. Do not join; mark beg of rnds.

Rnd 1: Ch 4, join to form a ring; 2 sc in each ch. *(8 sc)*

Rnd 2: 2 sc in each sc. *(16 sc)*

Rnd 3: Sc in each sc.

Rnds 4–18: Rep rnd 3.

Rnd 19: 2 sc in each of next 8 sc; sc in next 8 sc. *(24 sc)*

Rnds 20–23: Rep rnd 3.

Stuff with fiberfill and shape.

Rnd 24: [Sc in next sc, sk next sc, sc in next sc] 8 times. *(16 sc)*

Rnd 25: [Sc in next sc, sk next sc] 8 times. *(8 sc)*

Rnd 26: [Sl st in next sc, sk next sc] 4 times. *(4 sl sts)*

Fasten off and weave in ends.

Ear
Make 2.

Note: Ear is worked in continuous rnds. Do not join; mark beg of rnds.

Rnd 1: Ch 4, join to form a ring; 2 sc in each ch. *(8 sc)*

Rnd 2: 2 sc in each sc. *(16 sc)*

Rnd 3: Sc in each sc.

Rnd 4: Rep rnd 3.

Rnd 5: [Sc in next 2 sc, sk next sc, sc in next sc] 4 times. *(12 sc)*

Fasten off and weave in ends.

Nose

With black, ch 2; 4 sc in 2nd ch from hook.

Fasten off, leaving 8-inch end for sewing. Weave in other end.

Muzzle

Note: Muzzle is worked in continuous rnds. Do not join; mark beg of rnds.

Rnd 1: Ch 4, join to form a ring; 2 sc in each ch. *(8 sc)*

Rnd 2: 2 sc in each sc. *(16 sc)*

Rnd 3: [Sc in next 3 sc, 2 sc in next sc] 4 times. *(20 sc)*

Rnd 4: Sc in each sc.

Fasten off and weave in ends.

Finishing

Note: Refer to photo for placement throughout steps. Use tapestry needle to sew parts together and to work embroidery.

Step 1: With 8-inch end, sew Nose just above center of Muzzle. Stuff Muzzle lightly with fiberfill and shape. Sew Muzzle to front of Head.

Step 2: Sew Front Legs to sides of Body, working back and forth from side to side, to allow Legs to move.

Step 2: Sew Back Legs to bottom sides of Body, working back and forth from side to side, to allow Legs to move.

Step 3: Sew Ears to Head.

Step 4: With black yarn, embroider eyes on Head above Muzzle.

EASY

Finished Sizes

Instructions given fit baby, child and adult sizes, according to individual instructions and size of hook used.

Finished Measurements

Circumference: 14 inches *(baby)*, 18 inches *(child)*, 20 inches *(adult)*

Materials

For Baby Version
• Heavyweight fleece fabric:
  ¼ yd rainbow
• Size L/11/8mm crochet hook or size needed to obtain gauge
• Tapestry needle
• Fabric glue

For Child Version
• Heavyweight fleece fabric:
  ¼ yd each raspberry (A) and orange (B)
• Size M/13/9mm crochet hook or size needed to obtain gauge
• Tapestry needle
• Fabric glue

For Adult Version
• Heavyweight fleece fabric:
  ⅜ yd plaid (A)
• Cranston Fabri/Knit Precut fabric strips:
  1 package off-white (B)
• Size N/15/10mm crochet hook or size needed to obtain gauge
• Tapestry needle
• Fabric glue

Gauge

Size L hook: 10 sc = 4 inches
Size M hook: 9 sc = 4 inches
Size N hook: 8 sc = 4 inches

Instructions

Baby Version

Note: *Cut fleece in continuous strip, ½ inch wide.*

Row 1 (RS): With size L hook, ch 21, sl st in 2nd ch from hook and in next 3 chs, sc in next 16 chs, turn. *(20 sts)*

Note: *Remainder of Hat is worked in* **back lps** *(see Stitch Guide) only.*

Row 2: Ch 1, sc in first 16 sc, sl st in last 4 sl sts, turn.

Row 3: Ch 1, sl st in first 4 sl sts, sc in each sc, turn.

Rows 4–37: [Work rows 2 and 3] 17 times.

Row 38: Fold piece in half with beg ch edge behind row 37; ch 1, working in back lps of sc on row 37 and in unused lps of corresponding chs of beg ch at same time, sl st in each st.

Fasten off and weave in ends.

Assembly

Turn hat RS out. Thread tapestry needle with 16-inch piece of fleece. Weave fleece under 5th st from 1 end on every other row. Gather to close top of hat. Tie ends in a bow. Fold up bottom end of hat to form cuff.

Child Version

Note: *Cut fleece in continuous strips, ½-inch wide.*

Row 1 (RS): With M hook and A, ch 26 sl st in 2nd ch from hook and in next 3 chs, sc in next 21 chs, turn. *(25 sts)*

Note: *Remainder of Hat is worked in* **back lps** *(see Stitch Guide) only.*

Row 2: Ch 1, sc in first 21 sc, sl st in last 4 sl sts; change to B by drawing lp through; cut A, turn.

Row 3: Ch 1, sl st in first 4 sl sts, sc in each sc, turn.

Row 4: Ch 1, sc in first 21 sc, sl st in last 4 sl sts; change to A by drawing lp through; cut B, turn.

Row 5: Ch 1, sl st in first 4 sl sts, sc in each sc, turn.

Rows 6–33: [Work rows 2–5] 7 times.

Rows 34 & 35: Rep rows 2 and 3.

Row 36: Fold piece in half with beg ch edge behind row 36; ch 1, working in back lps of sc on row 36 and in unused lps of corresponding chs of beg ch at same time, sl st in each st.

Fasten off and weave in ends.

Assembly

Turn hat RS out. Thread tapestry needle with 16-inch piece of fleece. Weave fleece under 5th st from 1 end on every other row. Gather to close top of hat. Tie ends in a bow. Fold up bottom end of hat to form cuff.

Adult Version

Note: *For precut fleece strips, glue ends tog and roll in ball. For plaid fleece, cut continuous strip, ½ inch wide.*

Row 1 (RS): With N hook and A, ch 31; sl st in 2nd ch from hook and in next 3 chs, sc in next 26 chs, turn. *(30 sts)*

Note: *Remainder of Hat is worked in* **back lps** *(see Stitch Guide) only.*

Row 2: Ch 1, sc in first 26 sc, sl st in last 4 sl sts; change to B by drawing lp through; cut A, turn.

Row 3: Ch 1, sl st in first 4 sl sts, sc in each sc, turn.

Row 4: Ch 1, sc in first 26 sc, sl st in last 4 sl sts; change to A by drawing lp through; cut B, turn.

Row 5: Ch 1, sl st in first 4 sl sts, sc in each sc, turn.

Rows 6–44: [Work rows 2–5] 10 times.

Rows 45–47: Rep rows 2–4.

Row 48: Fold piece in half with beg ch edge behind row 47; ch 1,working in back lps of sc on row 47 and in unused lps of corresponding chs of beg ch at same time, sl st in each st.

Fasten off and weave in ends.

Assembly

Turn hat RS out. Thread tapestry needle with 16-inch piece of fleece. Weave fleece under 5th st from 1 end on every other row. Gather to close top of hat. Tie ends in a bow. Fold up bottom end of hat to form cuff.

EASY

Sizes

Instructions given fit baby, child and adult sizes, according to individual instructions and size of hook used.

Finished Measurements

4 x 23 inches *(baby);* 4 x 31 inches, excluding Fringe *(child);* 5 x 44 inches, excluding Fringe *(adult)*

Materials

For Baby Version
• Heavyweight fleece fabric:
  ¼ yd rainbow
• Size L/11/8mm crochet hook or size needed to obtain gauge
• Tapestry needle
• Fabric glue

For Child Version
• Heavyweight fleece fabric:
  ¼ yd each raspberry (A) and orange (B)
• Size M/13/9mm crochet hook or size needed to obtain gauge
• Tapestry needle
• Fabric glue

For Adult Version
• Heavyweight fleece fabric:
  ⅜ yd plaid (A)
• Cranston Fabri/Knit Precut fabric strips:
  1 package off-white (B)
• Size N/15/10mm crochet hook or size needed to obtain gauge
• Tapestry needle
• Fabric glue

Gauge

Size L hook: 10 sc = 4 inches
Size M hook: 9 sc = 4 inches
Size N hook: 8 sc = 4 inches

Instructions

Baby Version

Note: *Cut fleece in continuous strip, ½ inch wide. Buttons and button lps are optional.*

Row 1 (RS): With L hook, ch 61, sc in 2nd ch from hook and in next 19 chs, sl st in next 20 chs, sc in each rem ch, turn. *(60 sts)*

Note: *Remainder of Scarf is worked in* **back lps** *(see Stitch Guide) only.*

Row 2: Ch 1, sc in first 20 sc, sl st in next 20 sc, sc in each rem sc, turn.

Rows 3–10: Rep row 2.

Fasten off and weave in ends.

Button
Make 3.

With L hook, ch 2; 2 sc in 2nd ch from hook; sl st in 2nd ch.

Fasten off and weave in ends.

Button Loops

Hold piece with RS facing you and beg ch to right; with L hook, join fleece in end of row 1; working across side, sl st in end of each rem row; working across next side, sl st in each st; working across next side in ends of rows, sl st in each row; working across next side in unused lps of beg ch, sl st in each lp to last 18 lps; [ch 5—*button lp made,* sk next 2 lps, sl st in next 3 lps] twice; ch 5—*button lp made;* sk next lp, sl st in each rem lp; join in first sl st.

Fasten off and weave in ends.

Finishing

Sew buttons opposite button lps.

Child Version

Note: *Cut fleece in continuous strip, ½ inch wide. Buttons and button lps are optional.*

Row 1 (RS): With M hook and B, ch 81, sc in 2nd ch from hook and in next 24 chs, sl st in next 30 chs, sc in each rem ch; change to A by drawing lp through; cut B, turn. *(80 sts)*

Note: *Remainder of Scarf is worked in* **back lps** *(see Stitch Guide) only.*

Row 2: Ch 1, sc in first 25 sc, sl st in next 30 sc, sc in each rem sc, turn.

Row 3: Rep row 2, changing to B at end of row; cut A.

Row 4: Rep row 2.

Row 5: Rep row 2, changing to A at end of row; cut B.

Rows 6 & 7: Rep rows 2 and 3.

Rows 8 & 9: Rep row 2.

Fasten off and weave in ends.

Button
Make 3.

With M hook and B, ch 2; 3 sc in 2nd ch from hook; sl st in 2nd ch.

Fasten off and weave in ends.

Button Loops

Hold piece with RS facing you and beg ch to right; with M hook, join B in end of row 1; working across side, sl st in end of each rem row; working across next side, sl st in each st; working across next side in ends of rows, sl st in each row; working across next side in unused lps of beg ch, sl st in each lp to last 27 lps; [ch 5—*button lp made,* sk next 2 lps, sl st in next 3 lps] twice; ch 5—*button lp made;* sk next 2 lps, sl st in each rem lp; join in first sl st.

Fasten off and weave in ends.

Finishing

Sew buttons opposite button lps.

Fringe

Cut B in 4-inch lengths; use 2 strands for each knot of fringe. Fold strands in half; draw folded end from back to front through end of row 1 on either short end of scarf. Pull ends through fold and tighten knot. Tie knots in ends of row 4 and 8. Tie knots in same manner on opposite short end. Trim ends even.

Adult Version

Note: *For precut fleece strips, glue ends tog and roll in ball. For plaid fleece, cut continuous strip, ½ inch wide.*

Row 1: With N hook and B, ch 101, sc in 2nd ch from hook and in next 29 chs, sl st in next 40 chs, sc in each rem ch; change to A by drawing lp through; cut B, turn. *(100 sts)*

Note: *Remainder of Scarf is worked in* **back lps** *(see Stitch Guide) only.*

Row 2: Ch 1, sc in first 30 sc, sl st in next 40 sc, sc in each rem sc, turn.

Row 3: Rep row 2, changing to B at end of row; cut A.

Row 4: Rep row 2.

Row 5: Rep row 2, changing to A at end of row; cut B.

Rows 6–9: Rep rows 2–5.

Rows 10–12: Rep row 2–4.

Fasten off and weave in ends.

Fringe

Cut B in 10-inch lengths; use 2 strands for each knot of fringe. Fold strands in half. Draw folded end from front to back between ends of rows 2 and 3 on either short end of scarf. Pull ends through fold and tighten knot. Tie knots between ends of rows 4 and 5, 7 and 8, 9 and 10, and 11 and 12. Tie knots in same manner on opposite short end. Trim ends even.

Abbreviations & Symbols

beg	begin/beginning
bpdc	back post double crochet
bpsc	back post single crochet
bptr	back post treble crochet
CC	contrasting color
ch	chain stitch
ch-	refers to chain or space previously made (i.e. ch-1 space)
ch sp	chain space
cl	cluster
cm	centimeter(s)
dc	double crochet
dc dec	double crochet 2 or more stitches together, as indicated
dec	decrease/decreases/decreasing
dtr	double treble crochet
fpdc	front post double crochet
fpsc	front post single crochet
fptr	front post treble crochet
g	grams
hdc	half double crochet
hdc dec	half double crochet 2 or more stitches together, as indicated
lp(s)	loops(s)
MC	main color
mm	millimeter(s)
oz	ounce(s)
pc	popcorn
rem	remain/remaining
rep	repeat(s)
rnd(s)	round(s)
RS	right side
sc	single crochet
sc dec	single crochet 2 or more stitches together, as indicated
sk	skip(ped)
sl st	slip stitch
sp(s)	space(s)
st(s)	stitch(es)
tog	together
tr	treble crochet
trtr	triple treble
WS	wrong side
yd(s)	yard(s)
yo	yarn over

* An asterisk (or double asterisk **) is used to mark the beginning of a portion of instructions to be worked more than once; thus, "rep from * twice more" means after working the instructions once, repeat the instructions following the asterisk twice more (3 times in all).

[] Brackets are used to enclose instructions that should be worked the exact number of times specified immediately following the brackets, such as "[2 sc in next dc, sc in next dc] twice." They are also used to set off and clarify a group of stitches that are to be worked all into the same space or stitch, such as "in next corner sp work [2 dc, ch 1, 2 dc]."

[] Brackets and () parentheses are used to provide additional information to clarify instructions.

Join—join with a sl st unless otherwise specified.

The patterns in this book are written using United States terminology. Terms that have different British equivalents are noted below.

U.S. Terms	U.K. Terms
single crochet (sc)	double crochet (dc)
double crochet (dc)	treble (tr)
treble crochet (tr)	double treble (dtr)
skip (sk)	miss
slip stitch (sl st)	slip stitch (ss) or single crochet
gauge	tension
yarn over (yo)	yarn over hook (YOH)

How to Check Gauge

A correct stitch gauge is very important. Please take the time to work a stitch gauge swatch about 4 x 4 inches. Measure the swatch. If the number of stitches and rows are fewer than indicated under "Gauge" in the pattern, your hook is too large. Try another swatch with a smaller size hook. If the number of stitches and rows are more than indicated under "Gauge" in the pattern, your hook is too small. Try another swatch with a larger size hook.

Skill Levels

BEGINNER
Beginner projects for first-time crocheters using basic stitches. Minimal shaping.

EASY
Easy projects using basic stitches, repetitive stitch patterns, simple color changes and simple shaping and finishing.

INTERMEDIATE
Intermediate projects with a variety of stitches, mid-level shaping and finishing.

EXPERIENCED
Experienced projects using advanced techniques and stitches, detailed shaping and refined finishing.

Stitch Guide

Chain—ch:
YO, draw through lp on hook.

Single Crochet—sc:
Insert hook in st, yo and draw through, yo and draw through both lps on hook.

Reverse Single Crochet—
Reverse sc:
Work from left to right, insert hook in sp or st indicated (**a**), draw lp through sp or st - 2 lps on hook (**b**); yo and draw through lps on hook.

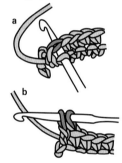

Half Double Crochet—hdc:
yo, insert hook in st, yo, draw through, yo and draw through all 3 lps on hook.

Double Crochet—dc:
yo, insert hook in st, yo, draw through, (yo and draw through 2 lps on hook) twice.

Triple Crochet—trc:
yo twice, insert hook in st, yo, draw through, (yo and draw through 2 lps on hook) 3 times.

Slip Stitch—sl st:
(a) **Used for Joinings**
Insert hook in indicated st, yo and draw through st and lp on hook.

(b) **Used for Moving Yarn Over**
Insert hook in st, yo draw through st and lp on hook.

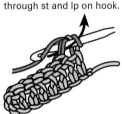

Front Loop—FL:
The front loop is the loop toward you at the top of the stitch.

Back Loop—BL:
The back loop is the loop away from you at the top of the stitch.

Post:
The post is the vertical part of the stitch.

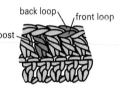

back loop / front loop / post

Overcast Stitch is worked loosely to join crochet pieces.

Standard Yarn Weight System

Categories of yarn, gauge ranges, and recommended needle and hook sizes

Yarn Weight Symbol & Category Names	1 SUPER FINE	2 FINE	3 LIGHT	4 MEDIUM	5 BULKY	6 SUPER BULKY
Type of Yarns in Category	Sock, Fingering, Baby	Sport, Baby	DK, Light Worsted	Worsted, Afghan, Aran	Chunky, Craft, Rug	Bulky, Roving
Crochet Gauge* Ranges in Single Crochet to 4 inch	21–32 sts	16–20 sts	12–17 sts	11–14 sts	8–11 sts	5–9 sts
Recommended Hook in Metric Size Range	2.25–3.5 mm	3.5–4.5 mm	4.5–5.5 mm	5.5–6.5 mm	6.5–9 mm	9 mm and larger
Recommended Hook U.S. Size Range	B1–E4	E4–7	7–I9	I-9–K-10½	K-10½–M-13	M-13 and larger

* GUIDELINES ONLY: The above reflect the most commonly used gauges and hook sizes for specific yarn categories.

Metric Charts

INCHES INTO MILLIMETERS & CENTIMETERS (Rounded off slightly)

inches	mm	cm	inches	cm	inches	cm	inches	cm
1/8	3	0.3	5	12.5	21	53.5	38	96.5
1/4	6	0.6	5 1/2	14	22	56	39	99
3/8	10	1	6	15	23	58.5	40	101.5
1/2	13	1.3	7	18	24	61	41	104
5/8	15	1.5	8	20.5	25	63.5	42	106.5
3/4	20	2	9	23	26	66	43	109
7/8	22	2.2	10	25.5	27	68.5	44	112
1	25	2.5	11	28	28	71	45	114.5
1 1/4	32	3.2	12	30.5	29	73.5	46	117
1 1/2	38	3.8	13	33	30	76	47	119.5
1 3/4	45	4.5	14	35.5	31	79	48	122
2	50	5	15	38	32	81.5	49	124.5
2 1/2	65	6.5	16	40.5	33	84	50	127
3	75	7.5	17	43	34	86.5		
3 1/2	90	9	18	46	35	89		
4	100	10	19	48.5	36	91.5		
4 1/2	115	11.5	20	51	37	94		

CROCHET HOOKS CONVERSION CHART

U.S.	B/1	C/2	D/3	E/4	F/5	G/6	H/8	I/9	J/10	K/10 1/2	N
Continental-mm	2.25	2.75	3.25	3.5	3.75	4	5	5.5	6	6.5	9

American School of Needlework®
excellence in instruction

DRG Publishing
306 East Parr Road
Berne, IN 46711

©2006 American School of Needlework

TOLL-FREE ORDER LINE or to request a free catalog (800) 582-6643
Customer Service (800) 282-6643, **Fax** (800) 882-6643

Visit AnniesAttic.com.

We have made every effort to ensure the accuracy and completeness of these instructions.
We cannot, however, be responsible for human error, typographical mistakes or variations in individual work.

ISBN-10: 1-59012-167-8
ISBN-13: 978-1-59012-167-2

All rights reserved.

Printed in USA

1 2 3 4 5 6 7 8 9